THERE WAS A TIME

TOMORROW MAY NEVER COME

CALEB MAINA IDI

THERE WAS A TIME
Tomorrow may never come

CALEB MAINA IDI

Table of contents

Chapter 1
Introduction

"There was a time, tomorrow may never come" is a phrase that speaks to the fragility and uncertainty of life. It conveys a sense of urgency to live in the present and make the most of every moment, because we cannot be certain what the future will hold. The concept of living in the moment is not a new one, and has been a central theme in many philosophical, spiritual, and cultural traditions throughout history.

In many ways, the phrase "there was a time, tomorrow may never come" is a reminder that life is fleeting, and that we should not take it for granted. We often assume that we will have a certain amount of time to accomplish our goals, pursue our dreams, and make a difference in the world. But the reality is that life is unpredictable, and we can never be sure what the future holds.

For many people, the idea of tomorrow not coming is a difficult one to contemplate. We often go through our daily lives assuming that tomorrow will be just like today, with no major disruptions or unexpected events. But as we have seen in recent years, life can change in an instant. Natural disasters, political upheavals, and personal tragedies can all disrupt our plans and force us to confront the uncertainty of the future.

In some ways, the COVID-19 pandemic has brought this reality into sharp focus. The pandemic has disrupted our daily lives, upended our plans, and reminded us that the future is never certain. We have been forced to confront our own mortality, and to consider what is truly important in life. Many people have used this time to reflect on their priorities, re-evaluate their goals, and make changes to their lives that will allow them to live more fully in the present.

Despite the challenges of the pandemic, there have been some silver linings. Many people have found ways to connect with others, even in the midst of physical distancing and isolation. We have seen acts of kindness and generosity that remind us of the best aspects of humanity. And we have been reminded of the resilience of the human spirit, as people have found creative ways to adapt to the new normal.

At the same time, the pandemic has also highlighted some of the inequalities and injustices in our society. The impact of the virus has been felt most acutely by those who are already marginalized and vulnerable. As we look to the future, we must work to address these systemic issues, and ensure that everyone has access to the resources and support they need to live full and healthy lives.

The phrase "there was a time, tomorrow may never come" also speaks to the importance of taking action in the present. We cannot control the future, but we can make choices today that will shape the course of our lives and the lives of those around us. Whether it is pursuing our passions, working to make the world a better place, or simply spending time with loved ones, every choice we make has the potential to create ripples that will extend far beyond the present moment.

Ultimately, the phrase "there was a time, tomorrow may never come" is a call to live fully and authentically, to embrace the uncertainty of life, and to make the most of every moment. It is a reminder that every day is a gift, and that we should use it wisely. By doing so, we can create a future that is more hopeful, more just, and more fulfilling for ourselves and for those around us.

Chapter 2
Embrace the Present

The present moment is all we truly have. It is the only moment that exists, the only moment we can experience, and the only moment we can act upon. Yet, many of us spend much of our time worrying about the past or the future, instead of fully embracing the present. In this chapter, we will explore why it is important to embrace the present moment and how to do so.

Why Embracing the Present is Important

Increases Happiness: By fully embracing the present moment, we can experience more joy and happiness in our lives. When we focus on the present, we can fully engage in activities that bring us pleasure and fulfillment, leading to a sense of contentment and satisfaction.

Reduces Stress: Focusing on the present moment can help reduce stress and anxiety. Often, stress is caused by worrying about the past or future, which we cannot control. When we focus on the present, we can let go of those worries and live in the moment, reducing stress and anxiety.

Improves Relationships: When we are fully present in our interactions with others, we can improve our relationships. We can listen more attentively, empathize more deeply, and connect more meaningfully with others.

Increases Productivity: By focusing on the present, we can be more productive in our work and other activities. When we are fully engaged in the present moment, we can work more efficiently and effectively, without distractions or worries about the past or future.

How to Embrace the Present

Practice Mindfulness: Mindfulness is the practice of being fully present and aware of our thoughts, feelings, and surroundings. It involves paying attention to the present moment, without judgment or distraction. By practicing mindfulness, we can learn to focus on the present and let go of worries about the past or future.

Engage in Activities that Bring You Joy: Engage in activities that bring you joy and fulfillment. Whether it is spending time with loved ones, pursuing a hobby, or simply taking a walk in nature, make time for the things that bring you happiness in the present moment.

Practice Gratitude: Practicing gratitude can help us focus on the present and appreciate the good things in our lives. Take time each day to reflect on what you are grateful for and express your gratitude to others.

Let Go of Regrets and Worries: Let go of regrets and worries about the past or future. Focus on the present moment and what you can do in the here and now to make a positive impact on your life.

Be Present with Others: When interacting with others, be fully present and attentive. Listen actively, empathize deeply, and connect meaningfully with those around you.

Practice Self-Care: Practicing self-care can help you be more present and focused in the present moment. Whether it is getting enough sleep, exercising regularly, or taking time for relaxation and self-reflection, prioritize self-care in your daily routine.

Take Breaks: Take breaks throughout the day to pause and focus on the present moment. Whether it is taking a few deep breaths, stretching, or simply taking a moment to appreciate your surroundings,

taking breaks can help you stay focused and
present.

Use Positive Affirmations: Use positive
affirmations to help you stay focused on the present
and positive in your outlook. Repeat affirmations
such as "I am present in the moment" or "I am
grateful for the present moment" to help you stay
centered and focused.

Chapter 3
Don't Procrastinate

Procrastination is a problem that affects many people. It is the act of delaying or postponing tasks or actions that need to be completed. In chapter 3 of this write-up, we will discuss the importance of not procrastinating and provide tips on how to overcome this behavior.

The Importance of Not Procrastinating

Procrastination can have a negative impact on many aspects of your life. Here are some of the reasons why it's important to not procrastinate:

Reduces Stress

Procrastination can cause a lot of stress. When you put things off until the last minute, you're more likely to feel overwhelmed and anxious. This can lead to poor performance, missed deadlines, and increased stress levels. By tackling tasks early, you can reduce your stress levels and feel more in control of your life.

Increases Productivity

When you procrastinate, you're wasting time that could be spent on other tasks. This means that you're not being as productive as you could be. By completing tasks early, you'll have more time to work on other projects and increase your overall productivity.

Improves Quality

Procrastination can also lead to poor quality work. When you're rushed to complete a task, you're more likely to make mistakes and overlook important details. By starting early, you'll have more time to focus on the task at hand and produce higher-quality work.

Boosts Confidence

When you procrastinate, you're putting off tasks that need to be done. This can lead to feelings of guilt and inadequacy, which can undermine your confidence. By completing tasks early, you'll feel a sense of accomplishment and boost your self-confidence.

Tips for Overcoming Procrastination

Overcoming procrastination is not always easy, but it is possible. Here are some tips that can help you overcome this behavior:

Set Realistic Goals

Setting realistic goals is important when trying to overcome procrastination. If you set goals that are too ambitious, you may become overwhelmed and give up. Start with small, achievable goals and work your way up.

Create a Schedule

Creating a schedule can help you stay on track and avoid procrastination. Make a list of tasks that need to be done and assign them specific times and dates. This will help you stay organized and focused.

Use a Timer

Using a timer can be a useful tool for overcoming procrastination. Set a timer for a specific amount of time and work on a task until the timer goes off. This can help you stay focused and motivated.

Break Tasks into Smaller Steps

Breaking tasks into smaller steps can make them feel more manageable. This can help you avoid feeling overwhelmed and make it easier to get started.

Eliminate Distractions

Distractions can be a major barrier to productivity. Try to eliminate distractions as much as possible when working on tasks. This could include turning off your phone or social media notifications, closing unnecessary tabs on your computer, and finding a quiet workspace.

Use Positive Self-Talk

Positive self-talk can help you stay motivated and overcome procrastination. Instead of telling yourself that you're a procrastinator or that you can't do something, focus on positive affirmations. Tell yourself that you're capable of completing the task and that you're making progress.

Hold Yourself Accountable

Holding yourself accountable can be a powerful motivator. Share your goals and progress with a friend or family member, or use a productivity app to track your progress. This can help you stay on track and avoid procrastination.

Reward Yourself

Rewarding yourself for completing tasks can be a great way to stay motivated. Set up a reward system that aligns with your goals, such as treating yourself to a favorite snack or activity after completing a task.

Practice Mindfulness

Practicing mindfulness can help you stay focused and present in the moment. Take breaks throughout the day to breathe deeply and clear your mind. This can help you avoid distractions and stay focused on the task at hand.

Don't Beat Yourself Up

Finally, it's important to be kind to yourself and avoid beating yourself up for procrastinating. Everyone struggles with procrastination at times, and it's important to remember that it's a normal behavior. Instead of focusing on past mistakes, focus on moving forward and making progress.

Chapter 5
Set Goals

Goal setting is an essential component of success, and it is the process of identifying what you want to achieve and determining a plan of action to accomplish it. Goals help individuals and organizations to focus their efforts and resources on the things that matter most, and they provide a roadmap for achieving success.

In this chapter, we will explore the importance of goal setting, the benefits of setting goals, and some practical tips for setting and achieving your goals.

Why is Goal Setting Important?

Goal setting is important for several reasons.

First, it provides direction and purpose. When you have a clear goal, you know where you are going and what you need to do to get there. This clarity can help you to stay motivated and focused, even when obstacles arise.

Second, goal setting helps you to prioritize your time and resources. When you have a clear goal, you can identify the tasks and activities that are most important to achieving that goal. This focus allows you to use your time and resources more efficiently and effectively.

Third, goal setting provides a way to measure progress and success. When you set a goal, you can track your progress and see how far you have come. This measurement can provide a sense of accomplishment and motivate you to continue moving forward.

Finally, goal setting can help you to develop new skills and knowledge. When you set a challenging goal, you may need to learn new things or develop new skills to achieve it. This learning process can be a valuable experience that helps you to grow and develop as a person.

Benefits of Setting Goals

There are numerous benefits to setting goals, including:

Increased motivation: Setting clear and challenging goals can provide a sense of purpose and motivation to achieve them.

Clarity: Goals provide clarity and direction, helping you to focus your efforts on the things that matter most.

Prioritization: Goals help you to prioritize your time and resources, ensuring that you use them more efficiently and effectively.

Measurable progress: Goals provide a way to measure progress and success, which can help to boost your confidence and motivation.

Skill development: Setting challenging goals can help you to develop new skills and knowledge, which can be valuable for personal and professional growth.

Greater satisfaction: Achieving goals can provide a sense of satisfaction and accomplishment, which can lead to greater happiness and well-being.

Improved self-esteem: Meeting challenging goals can boost your self-esteem and confidence, which can have a positive impact on all areas of your life.

Greater resilience: Setting and achieving goals can help you to develop greater resilience and perseverance, which can help you to overcome obstacles and setbacks.

Practical Tips for Setting and Achieving Goals

Here are some practical tips for setting and achieving your goals:

Define your goals clearly: To achieve your goals, you need to define them clearly. Be specific about what you want to achieve, why it is important to you, and when you want to achieve it.

Make your goals challenging but achievable: Your goals should be challenging enough to motivate you, but not so difficult that they become overwhelming or impossible to achieve.

Break your goals down into smaller steps: To make your goals more manageable, break them down into smaller steps or milestones. This will help you to stay motivated and make progress towards your goal.

Create a plan of action: Once you have defined your goals and broken them down into smaller steps, create a plan of action to achieve them. Identify the tasks and activities that you need to do, and create a timeline or schedule to help you stay on track.

Stay motivated: To achieve your goals, you need to stay motivated. Find ways to stay inspired and remind yourself of why your goals are important to you. This could include visualizing your success, creating a vision board, or surrounding yourself with supportive people.

Track your progress: Tracking your progress can help you to stay motivated and focused. Keep a record of the progress you make towards your goals, and celebrate your successes along the way.

Adjust your goals as needed: It is important to be flexible and adjust your goals as needed. If you encounter obstacles or challenges, reassess your goals and adjust them if necessary.

Hold yourself accountable: To achieve your goals, you need to hold yourself accountable. This could mean setting deadlines, tracking your progress, or sharing your goals with others to create accountability.

Learn from setbacks: Setbacks are a natural part of the goal-setting process. Rather than becoming discouraged by setbacks, use them as an opportunity to learn and grow. Identify what went wrong, and use that knowledge to make changes and move forward.

Celebrate your successes: Celebrate your successes along the way, no matter how small they may be. This will help you to stay motivated and create a positive mindset towards your goals.

Examples of Goals

There are countless goals that individuals and organizations can set for themselves. Here are some examples of different types of goals:

Personal Development Goals: These goals focus on personal growth and development, such as improving a specific skill or learning a new language.

Career Goals: These goals focus on career advancement and may include getting a promotion, starting a new job, or developing new skills that are relevant to your career.

Financial Goals: These goals focus on achieving financial stability or achieving a specific financial milestone, such as saving for a down payment on a house or paying off debt.

Health and Wellness Goals: These goals focus on improving physical or mental health, such as losing weight, quitting smoking, or meditating regularly.

Relationship Goals: These goals focus on improving relationships with family, friends, or significant others, such as spending more quality time together or improving communication.

Chapter 6
Live with Purpose

Living with purpose is one of the most important aspects of a fulfilling and meaningful life. When we have a clear sense of purpose, we are more likely to feel motivated, focused, and engaged in our daily activities. A sense of purpose gives us direction and helps us prioritize our time and energy. In this chapter, we will explore the importance of living with purpose and how to develop a sense of purpose in our lives.

The Importance of Living with Purpose

Living with purpose is important for many reasons. Here are a few of the most important ones:

Provides Direction: Having a clear sense of purpose helps us to know where we are going and what we want to achieve. It helps us to prioritize our time and energy and focus on what is truly important.

Increases Motivation: When we have a sense of purpose, we are more likely to feel motivated to take action and work towards our goals. This motivation can help us overcome obstacles and push through difficult times.

Creates Meaning: Living with purpose gives our lives meaning and makes us feel like we are contributing something meaningful to the world. This can help us feel fulfilled and satisfied with our lives.

Helps with Decision Making: When we have a clear sense of purpose, we are better able to make decisions that are aligned with our values and goals. This can help us make better choices and avoid regret and disappointment.

Improves Mental Health: Living with purpose has been linked to better mental health outcomes, including lower levels of depression and anxiety. This may be because having a sense of purpose can help us feel more in control of our lives and give us a sense of hope and optimism.

How to Develop a Sense of Purpose

If you are feeling lost or lacking a sense of purpose in your life, don't worry – it's never too late to develop a sense of purpose. Here are some strategies that can help:

Reflect on Your Values: Start by reflecting on your values and what is truly important to you. What do you believe in? What are your priorities? These values can help guide you in developing a sense of purpose.

Identify Your Strengths: What are your strengths and talents? What are you good at? These strengths can help you identify areas where you can make a meaningful contribution.

Consider Your Passions: What do you love to do? What activities bring you joy and fulfillment? Pursuing your passions can be a powerful way to develop a sense of purpose.

Set Goals: Once you have a sense of your values, strengths, and passions, set some goals that align with these things. Having specific goals can help you stay motivated and focused.

Serve Others: Helping others can be a powerful way to develop a sense of purpose. Consider volunteering, donating to charity, or finding ways to help those in need in your community.

Embrace Challenges: Challenges and setbacks are a natural part of life, but they can also be opportunities for growth and learning. Embrace challenges as opportunities to develop new skills and strengths.

Take Action: Finally, take action towards your goals and purpose. Start small, but take consistent steps towards your goals. Every action you take can help you feel more in control of your life and more connected to your purpose.

Examples of Living with Purpose

Here are some examples of people who have lived with purpose:

Mahatma Gandhi: Gandhi is perhaps one of the most well-known examples of living with purpose. He dedicated his life to the pursuit of justice and equality, using non-violent resistance to fight against British rule in India.

Mother Teresa: Mother Teresa was a Catholic nun who devoted her life to helping the poor and sick. She founded the Missionaries of Charity, a charitable organization that provides aid to those in need around the world.

Martin Luther King Jr.: King was a civil rights leader who fought for racial equality in the United States. He used non-violent resistance to bring attention to the injustices faced by African Americans and inspired a movement towards greater equality and justice.

Malala Yousafzai: Yousafzai is a Pakistani activist who advocates for girls' education. She survived an assassination attempt by the Taliban in 2012 and has continued to speak out for the rights of girls and women around the world.

Elon Musk: Musk is a tech entrepreneur who has founded companies like Tesla and SpaceX with the goal of making the world a better place. He is driven by a sense of purpose to reduce carbon emissions and make space travel more accessible.

These individuals all had a clear sense of purpose and were driven by a desire to make the world a better place. They each used their unique talents, passions, and strengths to make a difference in the world and inspire others to do the same.

Living with Purpose in Daily Life

Living with purpose doesn't always have to involve grand gestures or world-changing actions. It can also involve small, everyday actions that help us feel more connected to our purpose and values. Here are some examples of how to live with purpose in daily life:

Practice Gratitude: Taking time each day to reflect on what you are grateful for can help you feel more connected to your purpose and values. It can help you focus on the positive aspects of your life and appreciate the people and things that matter most to you.

Be Present: Living in the present moment can help you feel more connected to your purpose and values. When you are fully engaged in the moment, you are more likely to be mindful and intentional about your actions.

Prioritize Self-Care: Taking care of yourself is an important part of living with purpose. When you prioritize self-care, you are better able to show up as your best self and pursue your goals and purpose with more energy and focus.

Connect with Others: Building strong relationships with others can help you feel more connected to your purpose and values. Surround yourself with people who share your values and goals and who can support and encourage you on your journey.

Find Meaning in Work: Even if your job isn't your dream career, you can still find meaning and purpose in your work. Look for ways to connect your work to your values and passions, and find opportunities to make a positive impact on those around you.

Living with purpose is an ongoing process that requires regular reflection, action, and self-care. By taking the time to develop a sense of purpose and prioritize the things that matter most to you, you can create a life that is fulfilling, meaningful, and aligned with your values and goals.

Chapter 7
Practice Gratitude

Gratitude is the practice of acknowledging and appreciating the good things in life. It is a powerful tool for improving mental health, increasing happiness, and building stronger relationships. Gratitude can be expressed in many ways, such as writing a thank-you note, saying thank you, or simply taking a moment to reflect on the good things in life. This essay explores the importance of gratitude, its benefits, and how to cultivate a grateful mindset.

Importance of Gratitude

Gratitude is essential to our well-being. When we focus on what we are grateful for, we shift our attention away from negative thoughts and emotions. This can help reduce stress and anxiety, improve our mood, and increase our overall sense of happiness and well-being. Furthermore, practicing gratitude can help us build stronger relationships by strengthening our social connections and promoting empathy and understanding.

Research has shown that people who practice gratitude regularly are happier, healthier, and more resilient than those who do not. For example, one study found that people who wrote down things they were grateful for each day reported feeling more optimistic and satisfied with their lives than those who did not. Another study found that gratitude was associated with better physical health, including lower blood pressure and better sleep quality.

Benefits of Gratitude

Gratitude has numerous benefits, including:

Improved Mental Health: Gratitude can improve mental health by reducing symptoms of depression and anxiety. By focusing on the good things in life, we are better able to cope with stress and negative emotions. Furthermore, gratitude can help us build resilience by reminding us of our strengths and resources.

Increased Happiness: Gratitude is strongly linked to increased happiness. People who regularly practice gratitude report feeling more positive emotions and greater life satisfaction than those who do not. This is likely due to the fact that gratitude helps us focus on the good things in life, which can help us feel more content and fulfilled.

Improved Relationships: Gratitude can also improve our relationships by promoting empathy and understanding. When we express gratitude, we show appreciation for the people in our lives and acknowledge their contributions to our well-being. This can help strengthen our social connections and foster a greater sense of community.

Better Physical Health: Gratitude has been linked to better physical health, including lower blood pressure, improved sleep quality, and a stronger immune system. This may be due to the fact that gratitude reduces stress and promotes positive emotions, which can have a beneficial effect on the body.

Cultivating a Grateful Mindset

Cultivating a grateful mindset is an ongoing practice that requires effort and intention. Here are some ways to cultivate gratitude:

Keep a Gratitude Journal: One way to cultivate gratitude is to keep a gratitude journal. Each day, write down three things you are grateful for. These can be small things, such as a beautiful sunset or a kind word from a friend, or larger things, such as a promotion at work or a healthy family.

Practice Mindfulness: Mindfulness is the practice of being present and fully engaged in the moment. By practicing mindfulness, we can become more aware of the good things in life and learn to appreciate them more fully. Take a few moments each day to focus on your breath and observe the world around you with curiosity and openness.

Express Gratitude: Expressing gratitude to others can be a powerful way to cultivate a grateful mindset. Take time to thank the people in your life for their contributions, whether it's a colleague who helped you with a project or a family member who always supports you.

Reframe Negative Thoughts: When we experience negative thoughts or emotions, we can reframe them by focusing on what we are grateful for. For example, if you are feeling stressed about a deadline at work, take a moment to be grateful for the opportunity to do meaningful work and contribute to your company's success. Reframing negative thoughts in this way can help shift your mindset from one of negativity and stress to one of positivity and gratitude.

Volunteer: Volunteering is a great way to cultivate gratitude by helping others and giving back to your community. When we help others, we are reminded of our own blessings and can develop a greater appreciation for what we have.

Practice Gratitude with Others: Practicing gratitude with others can be a powerful way to build relationships and foster a sense of community. Consider starting a gratitude circle with friends or family, where each person shares something they are grateful for each day.

Use Gratitude Affirmations: Affirmations are positive statements that can help reprogram our thoughts and beliefs. Using gratitude affirmations can help us cultivate a more positive and grateful mindset. Some examples of gratitude affirmations include "I am grateful for all the abundance in my life" or "I am thankful for the love and support of my friends and family."

Challenges to Practicing Gratitude

Despite the many benefits of gratitude, there are some challenges to practicing it consistently.

One of the biggest challenges is our tendency to focus on the negative rather than the positive. We may be more likely to dwell on a bad experience or negative comment than to savor a positive experience or kind word.

Another challenge to practicing gratitude is our busy, fast-paced lives. It can be difficult to slow down and take the time to reflect on what we are grateful for when we are constantly rushing from one thing to the next.

Finally, it can be challenging to practice gratitude when we are going through difficult times or facing significant challenges. During these times, it can be hard to find things to be grateful for and to maintain a positive mindset.

Tips for Overcoming Challenges

Here are some tips for overcoming the challenges to practicing gratitude:

Focus on the Positive: Rather than dwelling on negative experiences or comments, make an effort to focus on the positive. Take time to savor positive experiences and appreciate the good things in your life.

Make Time for Gratitude: Set aside time each day to reflect on what you are grateful for. This could be first thing in the morning or before you go to bed at night. Even a few minutes of reflection can make a big difference.

Practice Gratitude During Difficult Times: Even during difficult times, there are things to be grateful for. Make an effort to focus on the positive and find small things to appreciate, such as a beautiful sunrise or a kind gesture from a friend.

Practice Self-Compassion: It's important to be kind to yourself and to ackMakenowledge that cultivating a grateful mindset is an ongoing practice. Don't be too hard on yourself if you have a difficult day or find it hard to focus on the positive.

Gratitude a Habit: The more you practice gratitude, the easier it will become. Make it a habit to focus on the positive and to express gratitude regularly. Over time, this will become second nature and you will naturally gravitate towards a more positive and grateful mindset.

Practicing gratitude is a powerful tool for improving mental health, increasing happiness, and building stronger relationships. By focusing on the good things in life, we can reduce stress, promote positive emotions, and cultivate a more optimistic outlook. Cultivating a grateful mindset is an ongoing practice that requires effort and intention, but the benefits are well worth it. Whether it's keeping a gratitude journal, expressing gratitude to others, or volunteering, there are many ways to cultivate gratitude in your life. By making gratitude a habit, you can transform your mindset and improve your overall well-being.

Chapter 8
Overcome Fear and Doubt

Fear and doubt are two powerful emotions that can hold us back from achieving our goals and living our best lives. They can prevent us from taking risks, trying new things, and pursuing our passions. However, it is possible to overcome fear and doubt and live a life of confidence and fulfillment. In this chapter, we will explore strategies for overcoming fear and doubt and living a life of courage and resilience.

Understanding Fear and Doubt

Before we can overcome fear and doubt, we must first understand what they are and how they affect us. Fear is a natural emotion that is designed to protect us from danger. When we perceive a threat, our bodies respond by releasing adrenaline, which prepares us to fight, flee, or freeze. While fear can be helpful in certain situations, such as when we are facing physical danger, it can also be debilitating when it is excessive or irrational.

Doubt, on the other hand, is a feeling of uncertainty or lack of confidence in oneself or one's abilities. Doubt can arise when we face a new challenge, are uncertain about the outcome of a situation, or feel like we lack the skills or resources to succeed. Doubt can prevent us from taking action, trying new things, and pursuing our goals.

While fear and doubt are different emotions, they are often intertwined. When we feel doubt about our abilities, we may also feel fear about the consequences of failure. Similarly, when we feel fear, we may doubt our ability to handle the situation.

The Impact of Fear and Doubt

Fear and doubt can have a profound impact on our lives. They can prevent us from taking risks, pursuing our passions, and living our best lives.

When we allow fear and doubt to control us, we may miss out on opportunities for growth and fulfillment.

Fear and doubt can also contribute to anxiety and stress. When we are constantly worried about the future or uncertain about our abilities, we may feel overwhelmed and anxious. This can lead to physical and emotional symptoms such as tension headaches, insomnia, and irritability.

Strategies for Overcoming Fear and Doubt

While fear and doubt can be powerful emotions, it is possible to overcome them and live a life of courage and resilience. The following strategies can help you to overcome fear and doubt and pursue your goals with confidence:

Identify the Source of Your Fear and Doubt

The first step in overcoming fear and doubt is to identify their source. Are you afraid of failure, rejection, or the unknown? Do you doubt your abilities or fear the consequences of taking action? By understanding the root of your fear and doubt, you can begin to develop strategies for overcoming them.

Challenge Your Negative Thoughts

Fear and doubt are often fueled by negative thoughts and self-talk. When you catch yourself thinking negative thoughts such as "I can't do this" or "I'll never succeed," challenge them with positive affirmations. Remind yourself of your strengths and past successes, and focus on the potential positive outcomes of taking action.

Take Small Steps

When facing a new challenge, it can be overwhelming to think about all the steps required to achieve your goal. Instead, break the task down into small, manageable steps. Focus on one step at a time and celebrate your progress along the way. This can help you to build confidence and overcome feelings of doubt.

Visualize Success

Visualization is a powerful tool for overcoming fear and doubt. Close your eyes and imagine yourself succeeding at your goal. Visualize the steps you will take, the obstacles you will overcome, and the positive outcomes you will achieve. This can help you to build confidence and reduce feelings of fear and doubt.

practice self-care to reduce stress and maintain a positive mindset. This can include exercise, meditation, spending time with loved ones, or engaging in hobbies or activities that bring you joy. Taking care of yourself can help you to feel more confident and resilient in the face of fear and doubt.

Seek Support

When facing fear and doubt, it can be helpful to seek support from others. Talk to a trusted friend or family member, a therapist, or a coach who can help you to identify strategies for overcoming your fears and doubts. Having a supportive network can help you to feel more confident and motivated to pursue your goals.

Take Risks

While it may be scary to step outside of your comfort zone, taking risks is essential for overcoming fear and doubt. When you take risks, you are challenging yourself and building resilience. Remember that failure is a natural part of the learning process, and each failure brings you closer to success.

Practice Gratitude

Gratitude is a powerful antidote to fear and doubt. When you focus on what you are grateful for, you are less likely to dwell on negative thoughts and feelings. Take time each day to reflect on the things you are grateful for, and focus on the positive aspects of your life.

Examples of Overcoming Fear and Doubt

Overcoming fear and doubt is a process, and it can take time and effort to develop the skills and mindset needed to succeed. Here are a few examples of individuals who have overcome their fears and doubts to achieve success:

J.K. Rowling

J.K. Rowling is the author of the Harry Potter series, one of the best-selling book series of all time. However, before she achieved success, Rowling faced significant obstacles and setbacks. She was a single mother living on welfare, and she faced rejection from numerous publishers before her first book was published. Despite these challenges, Rowling persevered and continued to write, eventually achieving immense success and acclaim.

Serena Williams

Serena Williams is one of the greatest tennis players of all time, with 23 Grand Slam singles titles to her name. However, Williams has also faced her share of challenges and setbacks. She has battled injuries, faced criticism from the media and her opponents, and dealt with personal struggles such as the death of her sister. Despite these obstacles, Williams has continued to work hard and pursue her goals, becoming a role model for perseverance and resilience.

Malala Yousafzai

Malala Yousafzai is a Pakistani activist and Nobel laureate who has become a symbol of courage and resilience in the face of adversity. Yousafzai was shot in the head by the Taliban in 2012 for advocating for girls' education. However, she refused to be silenced and has continued to speak out for human rights and education for all. Yousafzai's bravery and determination have inspired millions around the world.

Chapter 9
Learn from Failure

Failure is an inevitable part of life, and how we handle failure can determine our level of success and happiness. In this essay, we'll dive into the importance of learning from failure and explore some strategies for doing so.

Failure is Inevitable

One of the most important things to understand about failure is that it is an inevitable part of life. No matter how skilled or experienced you are, you will inevitably encounter setbacks, make mistakes, and experience failures. This is simply part of the learning process, and it's how we improve ourselves and grow as individuals.

Unfortunately, many people have a negative relationship with failure. They see it as a sign of weakness, incompetence, or inadequacy. They may feel ashamed, embarrassed, or defeated when they fail, and may even give up on their goals altogether. This is a dangerous mindset to have, as it can prevent us from taking risks and pursuing our dreams.

The Importance of Learning from Failure

So, why is it so important to learn from failure? For one, it can help us avoid making the same mistakes in the future. When we take the time to reflect on our failures, we can identify what went wrong and come up with strategies for doing better next time. This can help us improve our skills, our decision-making abilities, and our overall performance.

Additionally, learning from failure can help us develop resilience and perseverance. When we experience setbacks or failures, it can be tempting to give up or feel discouraged. However, if we can learn from these experiences and use them as opportunities for growth, we can develop the mental fortitude to keep going even when things get tough.

Strategies for Learning from Failure

Now that we understand why it's important to learn from failure, let's explore some strategies for doing so:

Reflect on What Went Wrong

The first step in learning from failure is to reflect on what went wrong. This involves being honest with yourself about the mistakes you made and the factors that contributed to your failure. Ask yourself questions like:

What did I do wrong?
What could I have done differently?
What factors were outside of my control?
Did I have the necessary skills, resources, or support to succeed?

Be as specific as possible when answering these questions. The more detail you can provide, the easier it will be to identify areas for improvement.

Identify Lessons Learned

Once you've reflected on what went wrong, the next step is to identify the lessons you can learn from your failure. This may involve looking for patterns or trends in your behavior or decision-making, or identifying specific skills or knowledge that you need to improve. Some questions to ask yourself include:

What did I learn from this experience?

What skills or knowledge do I need to develop in order to succeed?

What changes can I make to my approach next time?

Again, be as specific as possible when identifying lessons learned. The more concrete and actionable the lessons are, the easier it will be to apply them in the future.

Seek Feedback

Another strategy for learning from failure is to seek feedback from others. This can help you gain a different perspective on what went wrong and identify blind spots that you may not have been aware of. Ask for feedback from people who were involved in the situation, as well as from trusted colleagues or mentors who can provide objective advice. Some questions to ask include:

What did I do well?

What could I have done differently?

What mistakes did I make?

What can I do to improve?

Develop a Plan of Action

Once you've identified the lessons learned from your failure, the next step is to develop a plan of action for how to apply these lessons in the future. This may involve setting specific goals, developing new skills or habits, or adjusting your approach to a particular situation. Some questions to ask when developing a plan of action include:

What specific steps can I take to improve?

How can I measure my progress?

What resources or support do I need to succeed?

What obstacles might I encounter, and how can I overcome them?

Be sure to set realistic and achievable goals, and break them down into smaller, manageable steps. This can help you stay motivated and make steady progress towards your objectives.

Embrace a Growth Mindset

Finally, one of the most important strategies for learning from failure is to embrace a growth mindset. This means seeing failure as an opportunity for learning and growth, rather than as a sign of inadequacy or defeat. It involves believing that your abilities and intelligence can be developed over time through hard work and dedication.

To embrace a growth mindset, try reframing your failures as opportunities for growth and development. Instead of beating yourself up over mistakes, focus on what you can learn from them and how you can improve in the future. Celebrate your progress and accomplishments, no matter how small they may seem, and view challenges as opportunities to stretch and grow.

Chapter 10
Surround Yourself with Positivity

People, environments, and experiences we encounter on a daily basis have a profound effect on our mindset and outlook on life. In this essay, we will explore the reasons why it is important to surround oneself with positivity, the benefits that come with doing so, and some practical tips for achieving this goal.

Why Surrounding Oneself with Positivity is Important?

The people we surround ourselves with, the places we visit, and the experiences we have all shape our mindset and emotional state. If we are surrounded by negativity, we are more likely to feel down and discouraged. Conversely, if we are surrounded by positivity, we are more likely to feel uplifted and encouraged.

Negativity can come in many forms. It can be the negative comments of a colleague, the stress and anxiety of a toxic work environment, or the constant barrage of negative news in the media. These negative forces can chip away at our mental well-being and make it difficult to maintain a positive outlook on life.

On the other hand, positivity can come in many forms as well. It can be the encouragement of a friend or loved one, the sense of accomplishment that comes with achieving a goal, or the simple pleasures of life, like spending time in nature or enjoying a good book. Surrounding oneself with positivity can counteract the negative forces in life and help maintain a healthy and positive mindset.

Benefits of Surrounding Oneself with Positivity

There are numerous benefits to surrounding oneself with positivity. Here are some of the most significant ones:

Increased Happiness and Optimism: Surrounding oneself with positivity can increase feelings of happiness and optimism. Positive people tend to see the good in situations and focus on solutions rather than problems. This can lead to a more positive outlook on life and increased happiness.

Improved Mental Health: Negativity can take a toll on mental health. Surrounding oneself with positivity can counteract this by promoting a healthy mindset and reducing stress and anxiety.

Increased Productivity: Positive environments can be motivating and energizing. This can lead to increased productivity and a better overall work ethic.

Better Relationships: Positive people tend to be more approachable and supportive, which can lead to stronger relationships and a more fulfilling social life.

Improved Physical Health: Positive people tend to take better care of themselves, which can lead to improved physical health. This can include things like regular exercise, healthy eating habits, and good sleep hygiene.

Practical Tips for Surrounding Oneself with Positivity

So, how can we surround ourselves with positivity? Here are some practical tips:

Surround oneself with positive people: Seek out friends and colleagues who are positive and supportive. Limit time spent with negative individuals who bring down one's mood.

Create a positive work environment: If possible, decorate one's workspace with uplifting images or quotes. Surround oneself with positive coworkers who share the same values and goals.

Limit exposure to negative media: Limit the amount of negative news and media one consumes. Focus on positive stories and media that promote good news and human kindness.

Practice gratitude: Take time each day to reflect on the things one is grateful for. This can be done through journaling, meditation, or simply taking a few moments to appreciate the good things in one's life.

Engage in positive activities: Participate in activities that bring joy and happiness. This can include things like hobbies, exercise, spending time with loved ones, or volunteering.

Focus on solutions, not problems: When faced with challenges or setbacks, focus on finding solutions rather than dwelling on the problem. This can help maintain a positive mindset and promote a sense of control over one's life.

Practice positive self-talk: The way we talk to ourselves can have a big impact on our mindset. Practice positive self-talk by replacing negative thoughts with positive affirmations.

Take care of one's physical health: Taking care of one's physical health is a key component of surrounding oneself with positivity. This includes things like regular exercise, healthy eating habits, and good sleep hygiene.

Seek out positive experiences: Seek out experiences that promote positivity, such as attending concerts or events that align with one's interests and values.

Learn from negative experiences: While it is important to surround oneself with positivity, it is also important to learn from negative experiences. Use these experiences as an opportunity to grow and improve oneself, rather than allowing them to bring one down.

Chapter 11
Take Care of Yourself

Self-care is an essential aspect of a healthy and happy life. It is a simple concept that requires individuals to prioritize their physical, mental, and emotional well-being. Self-care can mean different things to different people, but it generally includes activities that help individuals manage stress, maintain a healthy lifestyle, and promote personal growth.

In this chapter, we will discuss why self-care is essential, the benefits of practicing self-care, and practical tips to help you incorporate self-care into your daily routine.

Why Is Self-Care Important?

Self-care is crucial because it enables individuals to take charge of their own well-being. In today's fast-paced and hectic world, it is easy to get caught up in the demands of work, family, and social obligations. Many people neglect their own needs in the process and end up feeling overwhelmed, stressed, and burnt out.

Taking care of oneself is essential to prevent burnout and improve overall quality of life. It helps individuals build resilience and cope with life's challenges. Additionally, self-care can boost self-esteem, reduce anxiety and depression, and promote better relationships with others.

Benefits of Practicing Self-Care

There are numerous benefits to practicing self-care. Here are a few of the most notable:

Improved Physical Health

Practicing self-care can improve physical health by reducing stress levels, promoting better sleep, and encouraging healthy habits such as exercise and a balanced diet. Studies have shown that individuals who practice self-care have lower rates of chronic diseases such as obesity, diabetes, and heart disease.

Better Mental Health

Self-care can help individuals manage stress, anxiety, and depression. Activities such as meditation, mindfulness, and journaling have been shown to be effective in reducing symptoms of anxiety and depression.

Increased Productivity

When individuals prioritize self-care, they are better able to focus and concentrate on their work. This can lead to increased productivity and better performance at work.

Improved Relationships

Self-care can improve relationships with others by reducing stress levels and promoting a positive outlook. When individuals feel good about themselves, they are more likely to have healthy relationships with others.

Practical Tips for Incorporating Self-Care into Your Daily Routine

Incorporating self-care into your daily routine doesn't have to be complicated or time-consuming. Here are a few practical tips to get you started:

Make Time for Yourself

Schedule time for yourself each day, even if it's just a few minutes. Use this time to do something you enjoy, such as reading a book, taking a walk, or practicing yoga.

Get Enough Sleep

Make sure to get enough sleep each night. Aim for seven to eight hours of sleep per night to help reduce stress levels and improve overall well-being.

Exercise Regularly

Regular exercise can help reduce stress levels, boost mood, and improve physical health. Find an exercise routine that works for you and stick with it.

Practice Mindfulness

Mindfulness practices such as meditation, deep breathing, and yoga can help reduce stress levels and improve overall well-being. Incorporate these practices into your daily routine to help manage stress and anxiety.

Eat a Balanced Diet

A balanced diet can help improve physical health and overall well-being. Focus on eating a variety of fruits, vegetables, whole grains, and lean proteins.

Limit Screen Time

Excessive screen time can increase stress levels and interfere with sleep. Limit screen time before bed and consider taking breaks from technology throughout the day.

Connect with Others

Strong social connections can improve mental and emotional well-being. Make time to connect with friends and family regularly.

Chapter 12
Give Back to Others

Throughout our lives, we are supported by the people around us in a variety of ways. Our parents provide us with love and guidance as we grow up, our friends offer us companionship and support, and our teachers help us learn and develop new skills. As we get older, we may find ourselves in positions of power and influence, with the ability to make a positive impact on the lives of others. Giving back to those who have helped us, and to those in need, is an important part of leading a fulfilling life.

Why Give Back?
Giving back to others is important for a number of reasons.

First, it allows us to show gratitude for the help and support we have received in our lives. We may have been helped by our parents, our friends, our teachers, or our colleagues. By giving back, we can show our appreciation and acknowledge the debt we owe to those who have helped us.

Second, giving back can help us develop a sense of purpose and meaning in our lives. When we help others, we feel a sense of satisfaction and fulfillment that comes from knowing that we have made a positive impact on someone else's life. This sense of purpose can help us find direction and focus in our own lives, and can lead to greater happiness and satisfaction.

Third, giving back can help us build stronger relationships with others. When we help someone else, we create a connection with that person that can lead to deeper and more meaningful relationships. This connection can help us build trust, empathy, and understanding with others, and can lead to stronger bonds of friendship and community.

Finally, giving back can have a positive impact on our own health and well-being. Studies have shown that people who engage in acts of kindness and generosity are more likely to be happy and healthy than those who do not. Giving back can help reduce stress, improve our mood, and boost our immune system, among other benefits.

Ways to Give Back

There are many ways to give back to others, and the best way to do so will depend on your own interests, skills, and resources. Here are a few ideas to get you started:

Volunteer: Volunteering is a great way to give back to your community and help those in need. There are many organizations that rely on volunteers, from food banks and homeless shelters to animal rescues and environmental groups. Look for organizations in your area that align with your interests and values, and reach out to see how you can get involved.

Donate: Donating money or resources to a charity or organization is another way to give back. There are many organizations that rely on donations to provide services and support to those in need. Look for organizations that align with your values and priorities, and consider making a donation to support their work.

Mentor: If you have skills or expertise in a particular area, consider mentoring someone who is just starting out in that field. You can help them develop their skills, build their confidence, and provide guidance and support as they navigate their career or personal goals.

Teach: Teaching is another way to give back to others. You can teach a class or workshop on a particular topic, or volunteer to teach at a local school or community center. Sharing your knowledge and skills can help others learn and grow, and can have a positive impact on their lives.

Listen: Sometimes, the best way to give back is simply to listen. Offer your time and attention to someone who is going through a difficult time, and provide a sympathetic ear and a caring presence. This can be especially important for those who may feel isolated or alone.

Random Acts of Kindness: Random acts of kindness are a simple and effective way to give back to others. You can perform small acts of kindness, such as buying a stranger a cup of coffee or leaving a note of encouragement for someone, or larger acts, such as organizing a fundraiser or volunteering at a local charity event. These small gestures can make a big impact on someone's day and can create a ripple effect of positivity in the world.

Impact of Giving Back

Giving back to others can have a profound impact on both the giver and the receiver. Here are a few ways in which giving back can make a difference:

Improved well-being: Studies have shown that people who give back to others are more likely to experience greater happiness, life satisfaction, and overall well-being. Giving back can help reduce stress, improve mood, and increase feelings of purpose and meaning in life.

Strengthened relationships: When we give back to others, we create a sense of connection and community with those around us. This can lead to stronger relationships and a greater sense of belonging.

Positive impact on others: Giving back can have a positive impact on the lives of those we help. Whether we are volunteering at a homeless shelter, donating to a charity, or mentoring someone in need, our actions can make a difference in the lives of others.

Social change: Giving back can also have a broader impact on society as a whole. By working together to address social issues, we can create a more just and equitable world for all.

Challenges of Giving Back

While giving back to others can be rewarding and fulfilling, it can also come with its own set of challenges. Here are a few things to keep in mind:

Time and resources: Giving back often requires a significant investment of time and resources. Volunteering, donating, and mentoring all require a commitment of time and energy, which can be challenging for those with busy schedules or limited resources.

Emotional investment: Giving back can also be emotionally taxing, particularly when we are working with individuals who are struggling with difficult issues. It is important to be aware of our own emotional limits and to take care of ourselves as we give back to others.

Balancing priorities: It can be challenging to balance our desire to give back with our other responsibilities and priorities. It is important to find a balance that works for us, and to be realistic about our own limitations.

Chapter 13
Embrace Change

Change is a fundamental part of life. It's inevitable and unavoidable. People can either resist or embrace change, and the latter is the more productive and positive approach. Change can be difficult and uncomfortable, but it's necessary for growth and progress. Embracing change means accepting that it's a natural part of life and using it as an opportunity to learn, grow, and improve. This chapter will explore the importance of embracing change and provide tips for doing so.

Why Embracing Change is Important

Personal Growth and Development:

Embracing change allows individuals to step outside of their comfort zones and try new things. It pushes them to learn new skills and develop new perspectives. It also allows them to identify areas where they need to improve and work on them.

Professional Growth and Development:
Change is an essential aspect of the workplace. New technologies, processes, and procedures are constantly being introduced. Those who are resistant to change risk becoming obsolete and losing their jobs. Those who embrace change, on the other hand, can position themselves as leaders and innovators.

Improved Adaptability:
Embracing change helps individuals become more adaptable. It allows them to handle unexpected situations and challenges with ease. Adaptable individuals are more resilient and better equipped to handle change in the future.

Increased Creativity:
Change often leads to new and innovative ideas. It forces individuals to think outside the box and come up with creative solutions to problems. Embracing change can stimulate creativity and lead to new opportunities and growth.

Improved Relationships:

Change can be a source of conflict in relationships. Those who embrace change are more likely to be open-minded and accepting of others' viewpoints. This leads to improved relationships and better communication.

Tips for Embracing Change

Acceptance:

The first step in embracing change is to accept that it's a natural part of life. No one can control or predict everything. By accepting change, individuals can let go of the fear and anxiety that comes with it.

Positive Attitude:

Having a positive attitude towards change can make a significant difference. Instead of focusing on the negative aspects of change, individuals should focus on the opportunities it presents. A positive attitude can help individuals approach change with an open mind and a willingness to learn.

Education:

Educating oneself about the changes happening can help individuals understand why they're happening and how they can adapt. It's essential to stay informed and up-to-date on changes in one's personal and professional life.

Flexibility:

Being flexible is critical when it comes to embracing change. Individuals should be willing to adjust their plans and adapt to new situations. Being rigid can lead to frustration and disappointment.

Seek Support:

It's essential to seek support during times of change. Talking to friends, family, or colleagues can provide a different perspective and offer emotional support. Seeking professional help, such as counseling or coaching, can also be helpful.

Take Action:

Finally, taking action is crucial when it comes to embracing change. Individuals should be proactive and take steps to learn new skills, try new things, and adapt to new situations. Taking action can lead to personal and professional growth and development.

Chapter 14
Live in the Moment

This concept can be difficult to define and even harder to put into practice. However, the benefits of living in the moment are many. By staying present and focused on the here and now, we can reduce stress and anxiety, improve our relationships, and find greater happiness and fulfillment in life.

In this essay, we will explore the concept of living in the moment in depth, examining its definition, benefits, and practical strategies for putting it into practice.

Defining Living in the Moment

Living in the moment is a mindset and practice that involves focusing your attention on the present moment, without worrying about the past or future. It means being fully engaged in what you are doing right now, whether that be a work task, spending time with loved ones, or enjoying a leisure activity.

Living in the moment means being fully present, aware, and mindful of your surroundings, your thoughts, and your feelings.

One of the main reasons why living in the moment is so difficult is because our minds are often preoccupied with worries, regrets, and anxieties. We may dwell on the past, replaying past mistakes or missed opportunities, or worry about the future, imagining worst-case scenarios or fretting about things we cannot control. Our thoughts may be so consumed with past or future concerns that we miss out on the richness and beauty of the present moment.

However, living in the moment is not the same as living impulsively or recklessly. It does not mean ignoring the lessons of the past or the responsibilities of the future. Rather, living in the moment means being fully aware of the present while also taking into account what you have learned from the past and planning for the future in a responsible and thoughtful way.

Benefits of Living in the Moment

The benefits of living in the moment are numerous and significant. Below are just a few of the many advantages of staying present and focused on the present moment.

Reduced Stress and Anxiety

One of the most significant benefits of living in the moment is reduced stress and anxiety. When we are fully present in the moment, we are less likely to worry about the past or future, and more able to focus on what we can control in the present. This can help us to feel more relaxed and calm, even in challenging situations.

Improved Relationships

Living in the moment can also help us to build stronger and more meaningful relationships with others. When we are fully present with the people we care about, we are better able to listen to their needs, understand their perspectives, and communicate our own thoughts and feelings in a clear and authentic way.

Greater Happiness and Fulfillment

By staying present and focused on the present moment, we can also experience greater happiness and fulfillment in our lives. When we are not distracted by worries about the past or future, we can fully engage in activities we enjoy, savoring each moment and finding joy in the simple pleasures of life.

Increased Productivity and Creativity

Living in the moment can also lead to increased productivity and creativity. When we are fully engaged in what we are doing, we are more likely to come up with creative ideas and solutions, and to be more efficient and effective in our work.

Practical Strategies for Living in the Moment

While the benefits of living in the moment are clear, putting this concept into practice can be challenging. Here are some practical strategies for staying present and focused on the present moment.

Practice Mindfulness

One of the most effective ways to live in the moment is to practice mindfulness. Mindfulness involves being fully present and aware of your thoughts, feelings, and surroundings without judgment. You can practice mindfulness by taking a few moments each day to focus on your breath and sensations in your body, or by engaging in activities such as meditation, yoga, or tai chi. Through mindfulness practice, you can learn to let go of worries about the past or future, and to focus your attention on the present moment.

Engage in Flow Activities

Another way to live in the moment is to engage in activities that promote flow, or a state of complete immersion in an activity. Flow activities are those that are challenging, but not too difficult, and that require your full attention and focus. Examples of flow activities might include playing a musical instrument, practicing a sport or physical activity, or engaging in a creative hobby. By fully immersing yourself in these types of activities, you can experience a sense of timelessness and deep engagement with the present moment.

Practice Gratitude

Living in the moment also involves cultivating a sense of gratitude for the present moment. Practicing gratitude can involve simply taking a few moments each day to reflect on what you are grateful for in your life, or actively seeking out opportunities to express gratitude to others. By focusing on the positive aspects of your life in the present moment, you can cultivate a sense of contentment and joy that can help you stay present and focused on the here and now.

Set Boundaries for Technology Use

One of the biggest obstacles to living in the moment in today's world is the constant distractions and interruptions of technology. To reduce the impact of technology on your ability to stay present and focused, consider setting boundaries for your technology use. This might involve turning off your phone during certain times of the day, limiting your social media use, or engaging in technology-free activities such as going for a walk in nature or spending time with loved ones.

Embrace Imperfection

Finally, living in the moment involves embracing imperfection and accepting the present moment as it is, rather than constantly striving for perfection or worrying about what could have been. By accepting the present moment as it is, flaws and all, you can free yourself from the burden of perfectionism and experience greater peace and contentment in the here and now.

Chapter 15
Conclusion

There was a time , tomorrow may never come . There was a time when the future was uncertain and tomorrow may never come. This phrase evokes a sense of urgency and immediacy, reminding us to live in the present moment and make the most of our time here on earth. Whether it be due to war, famine, disease, or personal circumstances, our ancestors knew all too well that life was fragile and unpredictable.

Today, we live in a world that is vastly different from that of our predecessors. We have made tremendous strides in science, medicine, and technology, allowing us to extend our lifespan and mitigate some of the risks that threatened our survival in the past. We have also developed a culture of consumption and instant gratification, which can distract us from the importance of living in the moment and cherishing the time we have.

Despite our progress, there are still many uncertainties and challenges that lie ahead. Climate change, political unrest, and economic instability are just a few of the issues that threaten our well-being and the well-being of future generations. Moreover, the COVID-19 pandemic has highlighted just how quickly our lives can be upended and how vulnerable we truly are.

In light of these challenges, it is more important than ever to heed the advice of our ancestors and live each day as if it were our last. This does not mean that we should be reckless or impulsive, but rather that we should be mindful of the choices we make and the priorities we set. We should strive to be present in our interactions with others, to express gratitude for the blessings we have, and to pursue activities and goals that bring us joy and fulfillment.

Living in the present moment can be challenging, especially when we are faced with the pressures and distractions of modern life. However, there are several strategies that can help us cultivate a greater sense of mindfulness and appreciation for the present.

One such strategy is to practice meditation or mindfulness exercises. These practices involve focusing on the present moment, typically by paying attention to the breath or to physical sensations in the body. By doing so, we can train our minds to be more present and less distracted by worries or concerns about the future.

Another strategy is to engage in activities that bring us joy and fulfillment. This could be anything from spending time with loved ones to pursuing a creative hobby or engaging in physical exercise. By focusing on the present moment and immersing ourselves in activities that bring us pleasure, we can cultivate a greater sense of purpose and meaning in our lives.

Finally, it is important to remember that we are not alone in our quest to live in the present moment. We are part of a larger community of individuals who are all striving to make the most of their time here on earth. By connecting with others, whether through social networks or in-person interactions, we can find support, inspiration, and a sense of belonging that can help us navigate the challenges of life.

In conclusion, there was a time when tomorrow may never come, and while our lives may be more secure and predictable than those of our ancestors, we still face many uncertainties and challenges. By living in the present moment, cultivating mindfulness and appreciation for the present, and connecting with others, we can find meaning, purpose, and fulfillment in our lives. Whether tomorrow comes or not, we can rest assured that we have made the most of our time here on earth.